First published in North America in 2006 by the
National Geographic Society
1145 17th Street N.W.
Washington, D.C. 20036-4688

Copyright © 2006 Marshall Editions
A Marshall Edition
Conceived, edited, and designed by Marshall Editions
The Old Brewery, 6 Blundell Street, London N7 9BH, U.K.
www.quarto.com

Trade ISBN: 0-7922-5893-2
Library ISBN: 0-7922-5894-0
Library of Congress Cataloging-in-Publication Data available on request.

Originated in Hong Kong by Modern Age
Printed and bound in China by Midas Printing Limited

Publisher: Richard Green
Commissioning editor: Claudia Martin
Art direction: Ivo Marloh
Picture manager: Veneta Bullen
Production: Anna Pauletti

Consultant: Professor Peter Jackson
Design and editorial: Tall Tree Ltd.

For the National Geographic Society:
Art director: Jim Hiscott
Project editor: Virginia Ann Koeth

One of the world's largest nonprofit scientific and educational organizations, the National Geographic Society was founded in 1888 "for the increase and diffusion of geographic knowledge." Fulfilling this mission, the Society educates and inspires millions every day through its magazines, books, television programs, videos, maps and atlases, research grants, the National Geographic Bee, teacher workshops, and innovative classroom materials. The Society is supported through membership dues, charitable gifts, and income from the sale of its educational products. This support is vital to National Geographic's mission to increase global understanding and promote conservation of our planet through exploration, research, and education.

For more information, please call 1-800-NGS LINE (647-5463) or write to the following address:

NATIONAL GEOGRAPHIC SOCIETY
1145 17th Street N.W.
Washington, D.C. 20036-4688 U.S.A.

Visit the Society's Web site at www.nationalgeographic.com.

Previous page: Marco Polo shown on a 19th-century medal made to celebrate his travels.
Opposite: A medieval illustration showing Niccolo, Maffeo, and Marco Polo leaving Venice by boat in 1271.

MARCO POLO

THE BOY WHO TRAVELED THE MEDIEVAL WORLD

NICK McCARTY

NATIONAL GEOGRAPHIC

WASHINGTON, D.C.

CONTENTS

A BOY IN VENICE

SETTING OUT

THE LONG JOURNEY

3

WORKING FOR KUBLAI KHAN

4

A BOY IN VENICE

1

Birth and Loss

Marco Polo is perhaps the most famous traveler who ever lived. We know the story of his journeys from the book he wrote, called *Le Divisament du Monde* (*The Description of the World*).

Previous page: The church of San Marco in Venice. St. Mark was the patron saint of the city. Begun in 1063, the church has five large golden domes.

Below: The city of Venice. In the background are trading ships, while gondolas are tied up at the quayside.

Marco's father, Niccolo, was a merchant based in the Italian port of Venice. In 1253, Niccolo's wife became pregnant. Niccolo and his family depended on trading, so he and his brother Maffeo set off on a trading expedition to Constantinople (now Istanbul in Turkey). In 1254, while he was still away, his wife gave birth to a boy who was named Marco. It is said that Marco's mother died very soon after he was born and that Marco was brought up by his aunt and her husband. We do not know if he had any brothers or sisters.

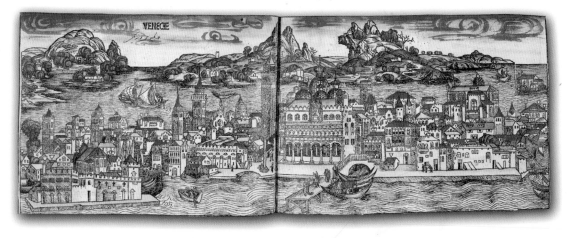

1234
Mongols from Central Asia invade and take control of the Jin Empire, which covered much of modern China.

1248–54
The Seventh Crusade begins. Venice makes money by supplying weapons and food to the Christian armies.

Below: In this courtyard, called the Corte del Milione, Marco Polo's family lived in a house like those in the picture. Their actual house was destroyed by a fire in 1596.

The Silk Road

This ancient overland route followed by the Polos stretches over 4,000 miles (6,500 km) from China to Europe. It became a series of tracks with any number of side routes to places where traders might profit. So the term "Silk Road" means any of the routes to places where silk, the most valuable item of the time, might be traded.

The years went by without any news of Niccolo or Maffeo. It was not uncommon for merchant adventurers who set off east never to return. Marco would have known that the life of a man like his father was full of dangers—from pirates, wars, disease, and floods.

As the son of a successful merchant and someone who would expect to join the family business, Marco would have been brought up in reasonable comfort. Venice was a rich city whose wealth was based on trade with countries around the Mediterranean and far away Africa and Asia. Men like Marco's father brought precious stones, spices, and much more into the city to trade with the rest of the world.

Merchants from all over the Mediterranean and beyond strolled across the city squares. No doubt Marco asked if anyone had seen his father and uncle. Marco was to be disappointed by their answers for many years.

1253

Niccolo and Maffeo Polo leave Venice for Constantinople.

1254

Marco Polo is born in the family home in Venice. His mother dies.

Niccolo and Maffeo's Story

In 1253, Niccolo and Maffeo sailed in a convoy of ships for Constantinople. This great city stood at the hub of trade routes—traders set out from there and traveled as far as India in the east and England in the west.

In 1259, after six years' trading in Constantinople, the brothers gathered together a store of precious stones and moved east into lands controlled by the Mongols. They may soon have wanted to go back to Constantinople, but a border dispute between two Mongol princedoms had broken out in an area directly between them and the city. They had no choice but to move on and to trade as they went.

Niccolo and Maffeo Polo traveled for weeks on end. They would have met other traders from time to time: Arabs, Greeks, Genoese, and others from Venice, like themselves. They were all trading in salt, furs, and slaves. But as the Polos moved farther from the main trade routes, the goods they preferred to trade were those that were easily transportable: gold, precious stones, and spices.

The slave trade

Thousands of men, women, and children from Europe and Asia as well as Africa were sold into the slave trade in slave markets from Venice in Europe to Timbuktoo in Africa and Bokhara in Central Asia. These slaves were sold to rich merchants and rulers in territories across Europe and the Middle East. Marco owned a Mongol slave called Peter. When Marco died, his will gave Peter his freedom.

1260
Kublai Khan is elected the Great Khan by agreement of the Mongol armies at Shang-du in China.

1260
Notre Dame Cathedral in Chartres, France, is completed. It is one of the greatest buildings of the Middle Ages.

Left: Niccolo and Maffeo Polo meet the great Kublai Khan for the first time. This is a miniature illustration made in Paris in 1412. European illustrators drew the Mongols with European features and pale skin because they had never seen anyone from Central Asia.

The Polo brothers moved into the land where Barka Khan, a Mongol leader, brought his people and flocks for summer pasture. The Mongol tents were pitched at Serai near the Volga River in an area now called Astrakhan. The Polos sold the stones they had brought with them for double the price they had paid. Barka Khan protected the two merchants and encouraged their trade. After a year, the brothers moved on to Bokhara in modern-day Uzbekistan. In the markets there they found porcelain, ivory, carpets, silks, metalwork, and more spices. Porcelain was made in China, and ivory, made of elephants' tusks, could also be found in the East. The rarity of all these goods in Europe made them very valuable. The Polos traded in the city for three years.

Then, by luck, they accepted the invitation of the local tribal chief, or khan, to go with envoys to meet the great Kublai Khan, ruler of the Mongols, who had defeated the Chinese and ruled most of their land. Marco wrote much later: "The Great Khan had never seen any Latins [Europeans] and had a great desire to do so." It was 1264, eleven years after Niccolo and Maffeo had left Venice, when they first met Kublai Khan in his palace at Shang-du in China.

1261

The Polo brothers stay with Barka Khan and then move on to Bokhara in Central Asia.

1261

The Byzantine Empire regains Constantinople.

School and Playtime

While his father was traveling, Marco was growing up in Venice.
We know very little about Marco's childhood. It is certain that, as the
child of a merchant trading family, he would have been taught the basic
tools of reading, writing, and enough arithmetic to add and subtract.

Marco might have been sent to learn to read and write in a small school
attached to one of the churches in the city. Or he might have learned these
skills from a clerk in the family trading house or from his aunt. After lessons,
Marco and his male cousins would then have been free to run wild beside the
canals and through the narrow streets and courtyards near their stone
house. When the boys were older they could row down the Grand
Canal, Venice's main waterway. In the square at the end of the canal
stood the church of San Marco, the symbol of Venice's wealth.

**Below: A modern version of the beautifully decorated
barge in which the *doge* (ruler) of Venice is still rowed
during the celebration of Ascension Day in Venice.**

1263
The Venetians defeat the Genoese in a
sea battle.

1264
Kublai defeats a rival for the title of
great khan, ending civil war.

Gamblers and traders lounged near the pillars on the waterfront. Marco might have stopped to stare at the dead or dying criminals executed there. He may even have tried to climb the walls around the Admiralty, where Venetian craftsmen built galleys, trading boats, and warships to order.

On feast days, the boys would have followed processions of the guilds and taken part in religious ceremonies. The *doge*, the ruler of Venice, was rowed in his magnificent red barge in an annual ceremony. He threw a gold ring into the waters as a symbol of the marriage of Venice and the sea. The youngsters would have joined in the parties and celebrations.

Life for wealthy girls in the Middle Ages was not so free. They would have been expected to stay in the house to help their mother with domestic duties. Children from poor families would have had no schooling and would have been expected to work at whatever they could find.

Above: In this stone carving, medieval boys are being taught their lessons.

Gondoliers

The boatmen who pole boats called gondolas through the canals of Venice are known as gondoliers. Legend has it that they are born with webbed feet. Their traditional boats are still handmade from as many as eight woods—beech, cherry, elm, larch, lime, oak, mahogany, and walnut. A new one can take three months to build and will today cost over $16,000.

1265
Niccolo and Maffeo Polo are taken to meet Kublai Khan.

1265
The great poet Dante Alighieri is born in Florence, Italy.

Venice

Venice is tucked into the northwest corner of the Adriatic Sea. In Marco's day it was the hub of a vast trading empire: trade routes stretched into Europe to the west, Russia to the north, Asia to the east, and across the Mediterranean to the Holy Land, Arabia, and North Africa. Venice was founded in the sixth century by refugees from the invading Goths, who were originally from Scandinavia. The refugees chose a site that was protected by the marshes and watery islands of the lagoon. Soon the Venetians began to replace their original wooden homes with more permanent stone buildings. To stop them from sinking into the lagoon, they made rafts of larch wood held in place by timber piles driven 25 feet (7–8 meters) into the solid mud at the bottom. These piles, packed tight, made platforms on which stone buildings could stand. They have lasted for hundreds of years.

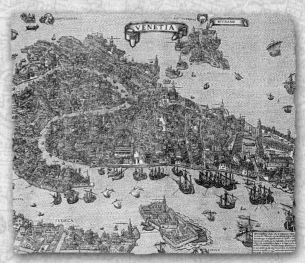

Above: A plan of Venice showing the line of the Grand Canal, ships in the lagoon, and outlying islands. The main "roads" through the city are wide canals like the Grand Canal or the narrower waterways connected to it, called *rios*. Every important building, even today, has a front door that opens onto water.

Left: This richly patterned glass plate was made on the island of Murano in the Venetian lagoon. Murano, and indeed the whole of Venice, is still famous around the world for its highly decorated glassware.

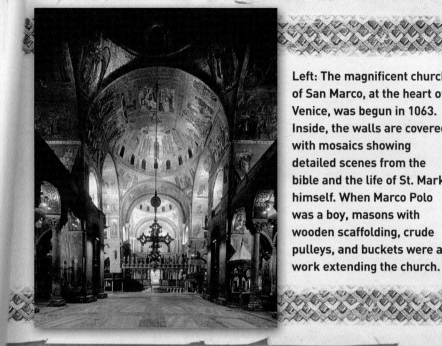

Left: The magnificent church of San Marco, at the heart of Venice, was begun in 1063. Inside, the walls are covered with mosaics showing detailed scenes from the bible and the life of St. Mark himself. When Marco Polo was a boy, masons with wooden scaffolding, crude pulleys, and buckets were at work extending the church.

Right: This highly ornamented binding held the statutes, or laws, of a Venetian craftsmen's guild. The image of a ship surrounded by a sunburst suggests that this was the statutes of a guild of shipwrights. In Marco's time, the craftsmen who made the boats, constructed buildings, blew glass, painted, made cloth, jewelry, wine, and all other goods, formed associations called guilds to protect their interests.

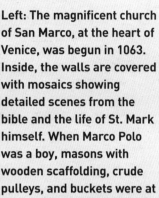

Niccolo and Maffeo Return

In China, the Polo brothers were welcomed by Kublai Khan, who was full of curiosity about the rest of the world. According to Marco, writing years later, "Above all he questioned them respecting the pope, the affairs of the Church, religious worship, and the belief of Christians."

Kublai Khan liked the Polos and he often asked them to come to his new court at Khanbaliq (now Beijing) during the two years they spent in China. Naturally, after all these years, the two men wanted to see Venice again. Kublai Khan gave them a passport after the brothers promised to return soon with a precious gift. The passport was a gold tablet which carried Kublai's seal. It stated that the Polos should be given everything they needed in all the countries they would pass through.

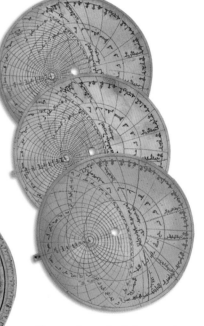

The brothers now faced a journey of thousands of miles across mountains and deserts. The journey was to take three years.

Above: An astrolabe made by an Arab craftsman in 1216. Astrolabes were used to work out the position of the stars and planets. Using this information, travelers could work out where they were and in which direction they should head.

1266
Kublai Khan makes the city of Khanbaliq (City of the Great Khan) his capital.

1268
Pope Clement IV dies. It takes three years for the next pope to be elected.

The brothers were continually held up by storms, snow, floods, broken bridges, and blocked mountain paths.

The two men had promised to take a message to the pope in Rome from Kublai Khan. But when they arrived in Acre, a port on the Mediterranean Sea, they heard that the pope was dead. So they decided that they might as well sail straight to Venice to see their families.

After years of wandering, the two brothers sailed across the lagoon, past the islands on its edge, and landed on the dockside in Venice, the bustling city they had not seen for so long. The year was 1269. Niccolo Polo did not know that his wife was dead or that he had a 15-year-old son.

Ambassadors to Europe

Kublai Khan was always curious about the world. He sent the two brothers home with messages for the king of France and the pope. He also sent with them a Mongol courtier as his ambassador. This courtier fell ill on the journey and the brothers were forced go on without him.

Left: A sailor navigates using an astrolabe (far left) in a medieval illustration. Sailors might also have used magnetic compasses, which arrived in Europe from China in 1187. They would have had simple maps, but sometimes the information on them would have been wrong, as map-making techniques were still simple and based to a large extent on guesswork.

1269
The Chinese landscape painter Huang Kung-Wang is born.

April or May 1269
Niccolo and Maffeo Polo return to Venice after an absence of 15 years.

SETTING OUT

The Merchants in Venice

Niccolo and Maffeo's homecoming, in April or May 1269, was not so much a rest as a pause. Before long, they planned their next journey to China. This time, they decided to take Niccolo's young son, Marco Polo, with them.

As the son of a trading family, Marco would probably have expected to go with his father on his next journey. If Niccolo felt he was too young, there is no mention of it in Marco's later writings. In the Middle Ages, boys were expected to start work much earlier than they do today. Niccolo would have been anxious to teach his son the skills necessary for trading in foreign countries. Niccolo, of course, had to get used to the idea that he had a son, and Marco had to get used to a father he had never met. Niccolo and Maffeo would have told the young man many stories of their travels.

Previous page: A medieval illustration showing a street where cloth- and furniture-dealers sell their goods.

Left: A stylized illustration of a nutmeg tree bearing its seeds, which were used for flavoring food. Nutmeg was brought all the way from India and was extremely valuable. On the right, a merchant weighs the seeds.

1270

The Eighth Crusade, led by Louis IX of France, sets off to recapture the Holy Land from the Muslims.

1270

The great painter Giotto of Florence is born.

Production line

A galleon built in Venice's boat yard, the Admiralty, could be fully equipped and launched in two hours. Once, a customer was shown a boat keel with some of the ribs in place. By the end of his lunch, the completed galleon was going down the slipway into the water.

Venice was like a huge warehouse for exotic goods from the east, from Africa to the south, and from the wild forests of Russia to the northeast. Silk, spices, and precious stones were the most valuable goods the Venetian traveling merchants brought home. Silk cloth found a high price in the cities of Europe. Spices were used to preserve everything from meat and fish to the embalmed bodies of the rich. Pepper, myrrh, incense, saffron, cloves, ginger, and nutmeg all found a ready sale in the markets of Venice, from where they spread throughout Europe. The precious stones were sold to expert cutters before finding their way onto the hands and necks of the wealthy.

Niccolo and Maffeo watched other traders bring back new goods to the warehouses. The brothers would soon have become bored with life in the trading houses in Venice. They were merchants first and last, and the brothers had not forgotten their promise to Kublai Khan, made over three years before.

Left: As today, merchants attracted customers by showing off their wares. Here a cloth-seller, possibly from Asia, is holding up a carpet.

1270
The Eighth Crusade is diverted to Tunis in North Africa.

1270
The Eighth Crusade is defeated by the plague. Louis IX of France dies at Tunis.

A Promise to Keep

The brothers were ready to return to China. They planned to sail first from Venice to Acre. There they had business with the papal legate, Theobaldo of Piacenza, who was on a crusade to take the Holy Land from the Muslims who ruled it. From Acre, if they got what they needed to keep their promise to Kublai Khan, they would travel on to China.

The gift that Kublai had demanded they bring back with them was no ordinary request. He wanted the brothers to bring the pope himself to Khanbaliq. They had explained that that might not be possible. He had agreed that he would accept a hundred Christian priests instead. He also wanted a quantity of the holy oil from the lamp that always burned in the Holy Sepulcher in Jerusalem.

Kublai Khan's mother was a Nestorian Christian whose tribe had been converted by one of the Christian priests who journeyed into the lands ruled by the Mongol tribes. Although he was a Buddhist, the Khan was eager to hear the Christian faith preached by European priests. Kublai Khan was a very broadminded man. In his court he gathered priests and monks from many religions. Buddhists, Muslims, Christians, and Jews all lived there.

Nestorian Christians

The Nestorian Church was a sect, or group, of Christianity which had spread across Asia. It had churches from Jerusalem to Khanbaliq. The sect was begun by Nestorius, bishop of Constantinople, in the 5th century.

1271
Prince Edward of England leads a crusade to Acre.

Summer 1271
The Polos set sail from Venice.

The only religions he refused to accept or to honor were those that demanded human sacrifice.

Pope Clement IV had died in 1268 and discussions about who should be the next pope had dragged on for three years. The brothers hoped Archdeacon Theobaldo of Piacenza, whom they knew, might be able to help them fulfill their promise.

Marco would have begun the exciting business of packing for a journey that had no foreseeable end. They had no idea how long they would be away. They would take bedding, food, cooking pots, water, wine, and a trunk of clothes onto the ship to Acre. They would also take salted meat, cheeses, onions, and garlic. Cooking on board was difficult as there was always a fear of fire on board wooden ships.

Right: The Church of the Holy Sepulcher was founded in the 4th century A.D. It is believed to be the site of Christ's burial and resurrection.

Summer 1271

Marco, Niccolo, and Maffeo reach the port of Acre in the Holy Land.

September 1271

Theobaldo of Piacenza is elected as Pope Gregory X.

How Marco Told His Tale

Marco Polo's book about his travels was written many years after his adventure. How did it come about? In 1298, Genoa and Venice went to war over who ruled the trade routes around the Mediterranean Sea. Marco Polo, now 44 years old, commanded a war galley for Venice. His ship was sunk and he was captured and imprisoned in Genoa. There, he told the tale of his travels in the East to a fellow prisoner, a storyteller called Rustichello of Pisa. The two of them decided to set the stories down as a book. When the war was over, Marco returned home with his manuscript.

Right: Copies of Marco Polo's book, *The Description of the World*, were written out by scribes and soon became very popular in Italy. The book was translated into English and French. The first printed copies were made in 1477. This title page of an edition of Marco's book was printed in 1529.

IL MILIONE

Marco Polo soon became known as "Il Milione," or "The Thousand," for the thousand lies some people believed he told in his book. Historians today still debate whether or not Marco Polo really did everything he claimed. He wrote about paper money, black stones that burned (coal), and galleys five times the size of Venetian warships. His 14th-century readers had never heard of such things and thought he was lying. Today, we know that these things were true. Marco also wrote about things that we cannot believe, such as birds that picked up elephants. The truth may be that Marco recorded not only what he saw but also stories he heard. Some historians argue that, if Marco really went to China, it is odd that he made no mention of the Great Wall. Other historians say that Marco only wrote about what interested him. He was a merchant and so he noted details about transportation, the economy, and trade.

Before the invention of printing, illustrated, hand-written copies of Marco's work were very popular. These illustrations were made around 1412 for a French version entitled *Le Livre des Merveilles du Monde* (*The Book of the Wonders of the World*). Below, Marco, Niccolo, and Maffeo say goodbye to their family at the city gate of Venice in 1271. On the right, Marco, Niccolo, and Maffeo leave a Middle Eastern town on their journey to China.

Setting Sail

The Polos set off from Venice's docks in 1271. Marco would surely have watched as Venice and all he was familiar with vanished over the horizon as the ship sailed across the lagoon. He would not see Venice again until 1295, 24 years later.

Above: In this medieval illustration, Marco, his father Niccolo, and his uncle Maffeo leave Venice by boat, not to return for 24 years.

The ship the Polos took was built both for speed and fighting. The front and back of the boat were built up almost like a fort from which the soldiers the ships carried could fight off pirates. Passengers were expected to carry weapons as well. The crews of these ships, only paid every three months or so, often stole what they could from the passengers onboard.

When they reached Acre, the Polos sought out Theobaldo of Piacenza. With his permission, they went to Jerusalem to collect the oil they needed from the Holy Sepulcher. When they returned, they hoped that a new pope might have been elected, but this had not happened. Only the pope could give permission to take priests to China, but the Polos decided that they had wasted enough time and set off anyway.

November 1271
The Polos leave Acre for Hormuz.

1271
Kublai Khan proclaims the start of the Yuan dynasty in China.

Right: Pope Gregory X, having just been elected pope, gives the Polos letters for Kublai Khan.

They had no sooner set off than Theobaldo himself was chosen as the next pope—Pope Gregory X. He recalled the Polos to Acre, where he blessed them and sent two friars to go with them to the court of Kublai Khan. They were instructed to teach Kublai Khan Christian belief. At last, the Polos could begin their journey.

They set off for the port of Hormuz, from where ships regularly sailed across the Indian Ocean to China. But nothing went according to plan. There were rumors of wars on their route. The friars were afraid for their lives; they refused to go on with the merchants and turned back home. The Polos went on their way without them. Niccolo and Maffeo believed they could explain their failure to bring the priests to the great Kublai Khan. Heading for the war zone, the Polos set off on the hard road south toward Hormuz.

Election of a pope

The election of a new pope was often a long process. All the cardinals gathered together behind locked doors in Rome and discussed which of them would be elected. The vote for the new pope had to be unanimous. Once a decision was reached, a fire would be lit and white smoke from the chimney announced to the world that a new pope had been elected. The same process continues to this day.

1271
The rulers of Egypt send a raiding party into Armenia. This frightens the friars traveling with the Polos.

1271
Prince Edward of England survives an assassination attempt in the Holy Land.

THE LONG JOURNEY

Traveling

On their journey to China, the Polos traveled across mountains and deserts, through dangerous floods, and past ancient cities. They traveled from Venice, the jewel of Europe, to Khanbaliq, the capital of Kublai Khan's empire. The city was greater than Venice in population, wealth, and even in organization.

Previous page: A camel train on the Silk Road, in a detail from a medieval map. An armed guard brings up the rear.

Below: The Polos arrive at a well-protected inn for the night in this medieval French illustration.

The route the Polos took was similar to a key track of the ancient Silk Road, which led from Europe to China. They carried their bags on the backs of donkeys, mules, horses, and camels. Sometimes they traveled with other merchants for safety, and sometimes alone.

1272
The Polos travel through Baghdad.

1272
The Polos are attacked by a robber tribe known as the Caraunas.

Some days they might make 20 miles (30 km), and on others no more than 5 or 6. So much depended on the terrain they were crossing and the weather.

At night, if they were lucky, they would arrive in an ancient town and find a *caravanserai* (an inn) where travelers could stay. Caravanserais were often little more than a low room built from stone. Walls in the yard offered shelter for the pack animals and the men who guarded them. These caravanserais also provided simple dormitories where people could sleep.

If they were still walking when night came, they could sleep under the stars or in leather tents made from the thick skins of animals. In drier places, they would look out for clumps of palm trees and vegetation where they would find water. These were called oases. Travelers would get together around them to tell stories, make music, and pass on news of the people they had met and the places that they had just passed through.

Food for the journey

The Polos carried flour with which they could make bread. On the way, they might hunt or fish. They cooked on fires made from charcoal or wood or even dried yak dung. They might buy cheeses made from local yak, sheep, or goat's milk. In the fertile valleys, they found fruit and vegetables.

The three travelers learned the various languages spoken by the people they met on their travels. These meetings with nomads, traders, and merchants in the markets they passed through gave the Polos the chance to ask for directions. Some of the route had been traveled before and may have been marked by stones. Using the sun and the stars, experienced travelers could keep going in the right direction. With the help of local knowledge, they moved with confidence through the countryside.

1272
Edward of England reaches a truce with the Muslims in the Holy Land.

1272
The Polos reach the port of Hormuz.

Serai

R U S S I A

Florence
Venice
Genoa
Pisa
Rome

Adriatic Sea

Black Sea

Caucasus Mountains

Aral Sea

Caspian Sea

TURCOMANIA
(ARMENIA)

Mt. Ararat

Baku

Bokhara

I T A L Y

G R E E C E

Constantinople
(Istanbul)

T U R K E Y

P E R S I A

Tunis

Mediterranean Sea

Mosul

Baghdad

Sava

Acre
Jerusalem

A F R I C A

A F G H A N I S T A N

Kerman

Persian Gulf

Hormuz

The Route

This map shows Marco Polo's journey
from Venice to Kublai Khan's capital at
Khanbaliq in modern-day China, which
took four years, from 1271 to 1275. It
also shows his journeys around Asia in the
services of the khan. In 1292, Marco set off
on his return journey from the port of Zaiton
(Amoy) on the coast of China. He eventually
arrived home in Venice in 1295. Historians
cannot be sure of the exact routes taken by the
Polos—the routes shown here are pieced together
from descriptions given in Marco's book.

A R A B I A

I N D I A N

O C E A N

When Marco Polo made his
journey, Europeans knew
little about the Far East.
Traders brought back
stories about Arabia and
India, but the lands farther
east remained mysterious.
People thought these
places were inhabited by
fantastic animals such as
the unicorn, shown with an
elephant, lion, and bear in
this illustration from an
edition of Marco's book.

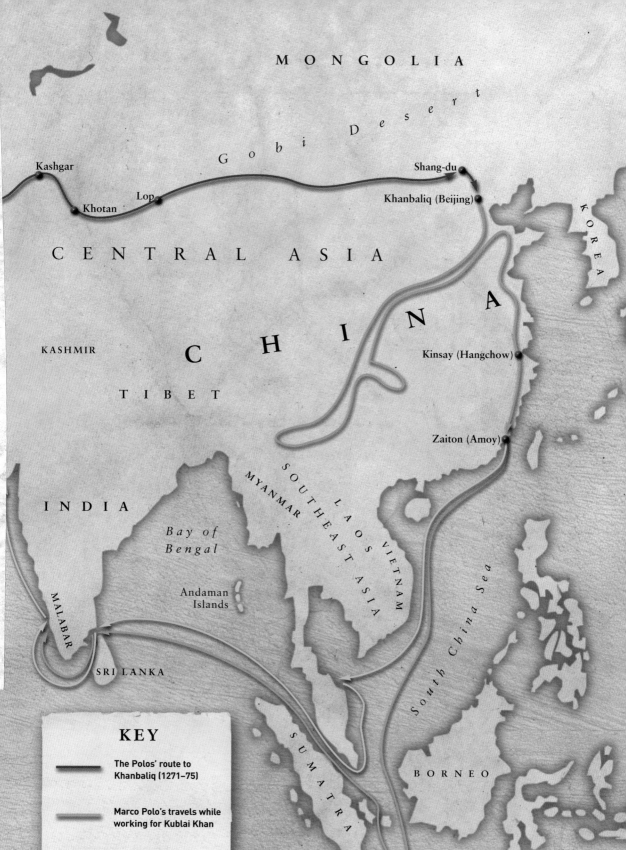

MONGOLIA

Gobi Desert

Kashgar

Shang-du

Khotan　Lop

Khanbaliq (Beijing)

KOREA

CENTRAL ASIA

CHINA

KASHMIR

Kinsay (Hangchow)

TIBET

Zaiton (Amoy)

INDIA

MYANMAR

SOUTHEAST ASIA

LAOS

VIETNAM

Bay of
Bengal

Andaman
Islands

South China Sea

MALABAR

SRI LANKA

SUMATRA

BORNEO

JAVA

KEY

The Polos' route to
Khanbaliq (1271–75)

Marco Polo's travels while
working for Kublai Khan

The Polos' route home
to Venice (1292–95)

The Road to Hormuz

As the Polos journeyed overland to Hormuz, Marco was fascinated by the different people they met, the places they passed through, and, most importantly, the goods for sale. He would later tell the story in *The Description of the World*. His natural trader's eye gives us a unique view of life in the Middle East during that period.

They traveled through Turcomania (modern-day Armenia), where according to Marco, "They weave the finest and handsomest carpets in the world."

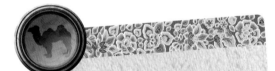

A horrible death

Once, Marco tells us, Baghdad was captured by Alau, Kublai Khan's brother. Baghdad's ruler had not protected the city, even though he had enough jewels to buy all the soldiers and weapons he needed. As punishment for the hurt he had done to his people, Alau locked the ruler up in a tower along with sacks of jewels. He told the ruler that since he loved his wealth so much he should eat it if he wanted to live. The ruler apparently died four days later with rubies stuffed in his mouth.

Beautiful handmade carpets are still made in that area today. They were often made on small looms which could be carried away when the tribe needed to move on to new pastures. These carpets were often quite narrow as a result.

The area south of the Caucasus Mountains was ruled by the Mongols of Persia, whose khan was an ally of Kublai's. Christians were allowed to worship in these areas, as were the Jews, Buddhists, Zoroastrians (fire worshippers), and others. Kublai was a believer in letting even people he had conquered worship as they wished.

1273
The Italian churchman Thomas Aquinas completes his work, *Summa Theologica*, which defines Christian belief.

1273
Edward I is crowned king of England in Westminster Abbey.

As they traveled south into Kurdistan, they passed Mount Ararat, where Noah's Ark was supposed to have come to rest after the world had been flooded. Marco didn't go and look for the Ark as "the snow on top of the mountain falls so constantly" that no one dared to climb up.

It was near here that Marco first heard the stories of black oil. "This oil is not good to use with food, but it is good to burn and cures the mange on camels," he wrote. These were the oil wells of Baku, which still pump out oil to this day. This is now made into gasoline.

They went on past Mosul, in modern Iraq, where Marco noted that many different races and religions lived—Arabs, Nestorian Christians, and Kurds—all ruled by Kublai Khan.

Below: Mount Ararat in modern-day Turkey, where Noah's Ark is said to have come to rest after the flood subsided.

1273
The Polos cross the region of modern Afghanistan.

1273
The Alhambra Palace is founded in Granada by Spain's Muslim rulers.

They traveled south through Baghdad (the capital of modern Iraq). Marco thought it was the most beautiful and "noble" city in the region and he commented on the wonderful carpets woven in the city. Trains of merchants bringing treasures from the east passed them. Their camel trains smelled of spices and scented woods, and rattled with jewels and elephant tusks. Even the pack animals were covered in silk and golden cloth.

Marco passed near the city of Sava in the Khanate of Persia, one of the four regions, or khanates, of the Mongol Empire. From there, legend has it, the Three Magi set out to worship the newborn Christ. Marco wrote with excitement, although he never saw it with his own eyes: "[The Magi] are buried here and their bodies are still entire with their hair and beard remaining."

In Persia, Marco noted a great supply of fine horses. He later wrote that "people take them to India for sale for they are horses of great price." Even a donkey could be worth 30 pieces of silver.

Right: A trading boat carrying livestock arrives at the port of Hormuz.

1273
The Polos travel through the Pamir Mountains in Central Asia.

1273
The Persian poet Jalal ad-Din Rumi dies.

"The fact is that in the summer a wind blows across the sand which is so hot that it would kill everybody were it not that when they see it coming they plunge into the water up to the neck until the wind dies away."

Marco writing of Hormuz in *The Description of the World*

The Polos came to Kerman, still in the Khanate of Persia, where they found many precious stones called turquoises in the mountains. Marco was particularly impressed by the exquisite silk embroidery created by the women of the region. Their work included "cushions and hangings and all sorts of things covered in flowers and birds."

Anxiously, the traders moved south through the land of the fearsome robber tribe called Caraunas. The Polos joined a larger caravan for protection against these dangerous men, but the caravan was overtaken by a dust storm and the robbers attacked in the confusion. The Polos escaped, but many others from the caravan were captured and sold into slavery.

After many months, the Polos arrived in Hormuz. In the harbor, they examined the Arab ships, called dhows, which were made without nails. The ships were held together by wooden pegs and with lengths of twisted twine. The Polos dared not trust themselves to such flimsy vessels to cross the Indian Ocean and round the coast of India to China. They refused to believe the Arab sea captains, even though Arab traders traveled hundreds of miles regularly in these boats.

Instead, the Polos turned their backs on the sea and decided they would make the journey overland. It was a hard decision, as they knew the route was through harsh and difficult country.

1274
The first attempted Mongol invasion of Japan ends in defeat for Kublai Khan's army.

1274
Marco Polo sees Mongols eating chopped raw meat mixed with garlic, today known as steak tartare.

Marco Falls Ill

The Polos doubled back on themselves toward Kerman, but this time sent guards ahead of them for protection against bandits. They then headed northeast into the area of modern-day Afghanistan and a vast salt desert.

It took eight days to cross the salt desert. No trees grew there, and the water was not only bitter but unsafe to drink. In the distance, the snow-capped Pamir Mountains emerged. As they toiled across the hot, dry plains, Marco became ill with fever. He was too sick to travel. No doubt they tried local herbal remedies and took advice from medicine men and women, but nothing cured him. As months passed, his father and uncle were impatient to move on. Finally, after a year, the Polos were advised to move Marco up into the mountains.

Below: A group of camels is dwarfed by the snow-capped Pamir Mountains. It was near here that Marco fell sick.

1274
Thomas Aquinas dies.

1274
The Polos trade for jade in Khotan, Central Asia.

Bucephalus

Bucephalus was Alexander the Great's (356–323 B.C.) favorite horse. He won it from his father, King Philip, by betting that he could ride the wild horse that no other man could even mount. Alexander, still a boy, walked to the horse and turned him gently by his halter so that the horse could not see and be frightened by his own shadow. He then vaulted onto the wild horse's back. Bucephalus was to go with him on all his military campaigns.

Above: This intricately inlaid pot was made in around 1200 in Khurasan in modern-day Afghanistan.

Marco later wrote that, if the people in the valleys fell ill with fever, they immediately climbed into the mountains for the excellence of the air. This treatment worked for him.

The mountains, with their pure air and streams full of trout, seemed like paradise after the sultry plains. There was other wealth to be found here, including a mountain where silver was mined. Alexander the Great, the 4th-century B.C. Greek military leader, brought his mighty army through these mountains. Legend had it that the beautiful horses there were descended from Alexander's favorite horse, Bucephalus. Marco recovered enough to note that the girls of the region "were the most beautiful [he] had ever seen."

From here, the travelers went south across the Hindu Kush Mountains and into Kashmir, but then took a route east toward China. They passed the jade mountains of Khotan, walked five days through sand, and finally reached the city called Lop. Here, travelers rested before they crossed the Gobi Desert.

1274

A church council regulates the election of the pope.

Winter 1274

The Polos rest in the city of Lop before setting off across the Gobi Desert.

Shifting Sands

The toughest test of travelers on this part of the Silk Road was the Gobi Desert. Stretching for hundreds of miles, even at its narrowest point, it took a month to cross. Legend held that the desert was haunted by *djins* (spirits) and that strange voices lured travelers to their deaths.

Resting in a caravanserai at Lop, Marco heard stories of the terrible hardship of crossing the dry, rocky landscape he could see from the edge of the city. It was said that winds blew the sand across the desert and wiped out all signs of tracks and paths. If you did not mark your path before you slept, it was likely that in the morning everything in the desert would have changed. But the Polos had no choice but to journey on. They set off across the barren land where men's minds could play tricks on them. There were no animals living there, and little or no water to drink.

Below: The trackless sands of the Gobi Desert, which the Polos crossed in 1275.

1275
Rebuilding work starts on the Tower of London, England.

Early spring 1275
The Polos cross the Gobi Desert.

Above: Niccolo and Maffeo Polo, on their knees, give Kublai Khan the bible sent by Pope Gregory X.

Marco wrote later: "Music wafts through the air and voices call the names of travelers and lead them into the trackless desert to their deaths." The music he described might really have been the howling of the wind through the rocks or even the sound made by shifting sand dunes. The Gobi was a fearsome place. The way across was marked by the bleached bones of the men who had failed to make it. By the time the Polos had crossed the desert, they had been traveling for nearly four years since leaving Venice.

Kublai Khan got news from his frontier guards that the Polos were coming and sent an escort on a journey of 40 days to meet them. These Mongol warriors greeted the Polos kindly and they were taken through northern China to Shang-du, Kublai Khan's summer palace, where the khan waited for them. It was May 1275.

The Polos prostrated themselves on the ground. Kublai was delighted to see them and asked them many questions about their journey. They were relieved that he didn't blame them for taking so long to keep their promise. They gave him the oil they had brought and letters from the pope. He was pleased with the gifts. Then he noticed the eager-looking young man and asked who he was. According to *The Description of the World*, Niccolo replied:

"This is my son and your servant, Sire."

"Then he is welcome too," said the most powerful of khans.

Spring 1275
The Polos reach the borders of the Empire of the Great Khan.

May 1275
Marco, Niccolo, and Maffeo reach Kublai Khan's summer palace at Shang-du.

WORKING FOR KUBLAI KHAN

4

In the Court of the Khan

The Mongol Empire was divided into four khanates. There was the Khanate of the Golden Horde in Russia, the Khanate of Persia, the Chagatai Khanate in Central Asia, and the lands of Kublai Khan in the east. Kublai, the most senior khan, ruled the Great Khanate, which spread from Korea to Tibet, south to Myanmar, and north to Lake Baikal.

Above: The great Kublai Khan (1215–94), leader of the Mongols in China.

Previous page: An imaginative 18th-century painting of Marco Polo dressed in Mongol costume. He holds the powerful curved bow used by the Mongols when hunting or at war.

The Polos were welcomed into Kublai Khan's court at Shang-du. There, in the middle of a vast hunting park filled with deer and other animals, Kublai Khan pitched his mobile palace. The palace, a huge and ornate tent held in place by silver silk ropes, was roofed with bamboo tiles lacquered in many colors. The khan was still a nomad at heart, like his ancestors who hunted the plains of Central Asia. He kept over 300 falcons (birds trained to hunt small animals) and an uncountable number of hounds.

In December, Kublai Khan and his court moved to the winter palace at Khanbaliq. Marco was astonished by the city's huge population and the general sense of order. Shops, workplaces for skilled goldsmiths, jewelers, tailors, potters, and porcelain makers each had their own area. The winter palace lay at the center of the city.

1276
Niccolo and Maffeo Polo are trading in China.

1277
Kublai Khan sends an army into the region of modern-day Myanmar and defeats the king of Mien in battle.

Left: Kublai Khan (center) hunting on horseback with members of his court, including a wife (with a white-painted face). This painting on silk was done by his court painter, Liu Kuan-Tao. Chinese arts were encouraged under Mongol rule.

Marco described the palace as being richly decorated with carvings and paintings. In the inner palace were the private rooms of the khan and his wives and mistresses. Each of his four wives had 10,000 servants and 300 ladies-in-waiting.

Marco described a well-ordered society in which Chinese governors ran their provinces with local councillors. The Great Khan, of course, had the final word. There was even a benefit system, set up years before by the Chinese, in which poor people were given food and clothes. In addition, there was a postal service that allowed letters to be sent 300 miles a day by a chain of horsemen set up for the purpose.

Kublai Khan

Kublai Khan was a dictator. He could be ruthless and would order a traitor to be executed without hesitation. However, he was also well known for his tolerance of other cultures and religions. When Marco met him he was 60 years old. His black eyes twinkled with humor. Like all his people, he loved horses.

1278
Kublai Khan allows Nestorian Christians to build three churches in the Great Khanate.

1279
Kublai Khan crushes China's Song Empire, becoming the sole ruler throughout China.

The Mongols

Above: The Mongols were originally a nomadic people, moving from place to place in search of hunting grounds and fresh pasture. In this 14th-century illustration their yurts (tents) made of decorated felt stand near a woman cooking over a fire.

The Mongols were a group of nomadic tribes who came from the plains of modern Mongolia in Central Asia. In the early 13th century, Genghis Khan, Kublai's grandfather, unified the tribes and started to create the biggest land empire the world has ever known. At its height, it spread from Korea in the east to Hungary and Turkey in the west. Russia, Poland, and Persia fell. Even China was eventually under their heel—200,000 Mongols ruled an empire of 100 million people.

Above: Genghis Khan (c.1155–1227) on his throne and surrounded by courtiers in this 14th-century Persian miniature. Genghis Khan was a cruel and pitiless ruler. He became leader of a federation of Mongol tribes in 1206. In less than 20 years, his armies overran the Muslim states of Central Asia and conquered much of northern China.

Right: Mongol armies were fast-moving and ruthless. The cavalry, in which each man was armed with two bows, an axe, and a sword, was devastatingly effective. Their tactics when besieging a city were simple. If the people refused to surrender, they burned the city to the ground. They would slaughter all but a few and let those few go free to warn others that death and destruction were coming.

THE MONGOL EMPIRE

KEY

EMPIRE OF THE GREAT KHAN

CHAGATAI KHANATE

KHANATE OF PERSIA

KHANATE OF THE GOLDEN HORDE

After Genghis Khan died, his descendants continued to expand the empire. Once they had conquered, they imposed law and order over the lands they ruled. The empire was stitched together by a magnificent communications system. Way stations were set up across the empire. Fresh riders were always ready in those way stations with spare horses. A message could go from Khanbaliq in the east to the Ukraine in the west non-stop. The Mongols were noted for their tolerance of the religions and customs of those they defeated. They originally worshipped the sky and forces of nature, but in China many Mongols converted to Buddhism. Like most nomads they created few artistic objects, but they encouraged the skills of the people they conquered. It was in these more peaceful times that Marco came to the court of Kublai Khan.

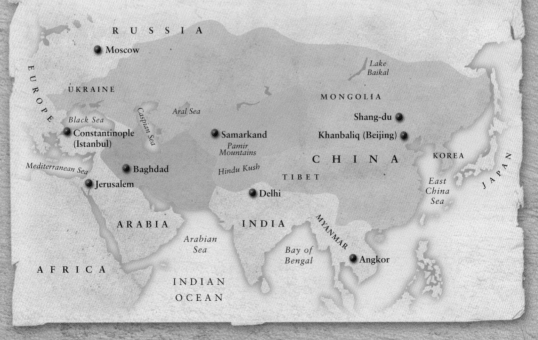

Marco the Spy

Above: Flaming arrows (shown here) were used by the Chinese against the Mongols. They may also have used gunpowder for the first time in their battles with the invaders.

Marco soon learned the customs and language of the Mongols and became a favorite of Kublai. According to Marco, the ruler was impressed with the young Venetian's quick intelligence. The khan decided to employ him as a traveling spy, acting as the ruler's eyes and ears in distant parts of his empire. Niccolo and Maffeo, under the khan's protection, went on working as merchants.

In 1275, Kublai Khan sent Marco on his first journey into the Great Khanate. On Marco's return to court, he would tell Kublai about the strange customs of the people he met. It was important for Kublai Khan to know everything because he was the ruler of a conquered country. Many of the people he was governing were not happy to be under foreign rule.

Marco went to the south of China. He traveled into what are now Myanmar and Vietnam. Forever on the move, he crossed the harsh interior of China to the busy coastal ports. He was often astonished by what he saw.

Circa 1280
Marco visits Vietnam.

1280
The court painter Liu Kuan-Tao paints Kublai Khan hawking.

"Every day as long as the body is not cremated they lay a table before the corpse covered with food and drink, sometimes for a matter of six months. The coffin being filled with camphor and spices to keep off corruption."

Marco writing about the funeral rites in northern China,
The Description of the World

He remembered and made notes about much of it. His book is the first detailed account of Chinese culture written by a European. Observations about the recording of births and details of local burials can be found in his book. He noted that when a Chinese child was born, astrologers would "write down the day and hour, the planet and star under which the birth has taken place. Astrologers say they can tell the future from this information."

There was so much for Marco to tell Kublai Khan on his return. The relationship between the two was like father and son.

Above: This blue vase with a white dragon design made in China during the Yuan dynasty is of the quality that would accompany a wealthy dead man into his grave for his use in the next world.

Circa 1282

The *Mappa Mundi* (Map of the World) is made in Hereford, England, showing the world as it is known to Europeans.

Circa 1285

Marco sets sail from Zaiton and travels down the coast of China.

Kublai Khan's mother

Kublai Khan's mother, Sorghaghtani Beki, was illiterate but understood the need to educate her sons. Each son learned the language of the area of empire he would rule. She made sure that each of them also was aware of the religions of the people they would rule. She made them understand that exploiting a conquered nation was not a good idea. It was her views that made Kublai Khan the great ruler he was. Religious toleration, support of the local economy, and keeping a close eye on Chinese officials were the keystones of Mongol rule in China.

The most astonishing passages in *The Description of the World* are those in which Marco describes the cities where Kublai Khan had his palaces. Kinsay (The City of Heaven), now called Hangchow, was magnificent. Like Venice, the city stands on and is surrounded by water. Here the comparison ends. Kinsay was 100 miles (160 km) in circumference and had 12,000 stone bridges that were so high that a fleet of ships could sail under each of them.

The city also had a total of twelve guilds of craftsmen who lived in 12,000 houses, each containing at least 12 workers. All of these highly skilled craftsmen worked constantly to make the gold and silver chains and jewelry, porcelain, pottery, armor, silk robes, and weapons to provide the inhabitants of the city with everything they needed. The streets of the city were paved and they had a covered drain built down the middle to carry away water and waste. Marco was astonished to discover that the people of Kinsay bathed as much as three times a month in one of the city's 3,000 communal baths, which were supplied by spring water. This was not what Marco was used to—back in Europe, a bath was a very rare event!

1286

Queen Bolgana dies in Persia.

1287

Kublai Khan's army overruns Myanmar.

Left: Divers collect pearls from the seabed off Malabar, in southwestern India, as described by Marco in his book.

Marco also heard of and saw other things that excited him. In 1285, he sailed from the port of Zaiton in a ship called a junk. He traveled past Java to the Kingdom of Basma on the island of Sumatra, where he saw or was told about animals he described as unicorns: "Nearly as big as elephants with hair like a buffalo, feet like an elephant, and a horn in the middle of the forehead." These were probably rhinoceroses.

From Sumatra he sailed to the island now called Sri Lanka. He went there to see an enormous statue of Buddha. He also saw a ruby owned by the king which was the size of a fist. Even Kublai Khan could not buy it. Marco described the sago tree, camphor, peppers, and the preparation of various spices. He sailed on to India and saw the pearl fishers of Malabar diving beneath the waves and heard about the supposed dog-headed men of the Andaman Islands who ate anyone they caught.

For 17 years, Marco Polo traveled, observed, and remembered what he saw as the eyes of Kublai Khan. His position, and his later fame, were dependent on his memory and the notes he made along the way.

1287
The first ever ambassador from Persia arrives in Europe.

1291
The Muslims capture Acre, the last Christian stronghold in the Holy Land.

Going Home

Kublai Khan was now 77 years old. Niccolo and Maffeo were growing older too, and they wanted to go home before it was too late. However, according to Marco's book, Kublai was not eager to let Marco go.

The three Venetians had bought many jewels with the profits they had made by trade. They were all wealthy men. They asked Kublai Khan a number of times if they could return to Venice, but he refused. The Polos knew that if he died they would be in danger and they might never leave. There were plenty of people in the court who were jealous of their friendship with the Mongol ruler. Fortunately, luck was on their side.

Queen Bolgana, the wife of Arghun, ruler of the Khanate of Persia and a great-nephew of Kublai, had died. Ambassadors from Persia brought the news that Queen Bolgana's last wish was that Arghun's next wife should be from her royal clan. Kublai Khan agreed that one of the royal princesses, Kokachin, who was 17 years old, was a suitable wife for his great-nephew.

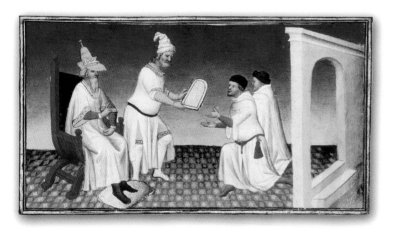

Left: Kublai Khan (far left) has an official hand the Polos their passport out of the Great Khanate.

1292
Persian ambassadors arrive in Khanbaliq with a message from Arghun, the khan of Persia.

1292
The Polos set sail from the port of Zaiton with Princess Kokachin.

Above: Mongol ladies such as Princess Kokachin would have worn jewelry such as this 14th-century bracelet.

The Persian ambassadors tried to return home with the princess, but warring tribes on the route made them turn back. They did not want to travel without an experienced guide. Niccolo and Maffeo met secretly with the ambassadors and offered their services. Marco had just come back from his journey to India, and the ambassadors were impressed with his seagoing experience. They asked Kublai Khan if the Polos could escort the princess to her husband.

The Great Khan ordered the Polos into his presence and finally gave his consent to leave. He gave them two gold tablets which acted as passports through all the lands he ruled. He organized a fleet of ships for them. These were equipped with everything they would need for the journey, which was to last two years. He made them promise to come back when the princess was safely delivered. After making preparations and gathering up their treasures, the Polos left China. Marco and Kublai Khan would never meet again.

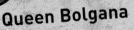

Queen Bolgana

Queen Bolgana was a very clever and beautiful woman. First, she was married to Arghun's father, Abaka. On his death, according to the customs of the Mongols at the time, she married his son Arghun. The girl who was to succeed her, Kokachin, was also beautiful, intelligent, and charming.

1292
Genoa destroys the Pisan navy to become Venice's chief trading rival in the Mediterranean.

1293
The Mongol expedition to Java to take over their spice trade ends in failure.

Above: The journey home was not without incident. Life-threatening storms were frequent. In this illustration from a French edition of Marco's book, two ships are battered by high seas as they pick up shipwrecked men near the island of Java.

In the port of Zaiton, the Polos found the 13 ships that had been made ready for them. Each of the huge four-masted ships had sixty cabins and a crew of up to 250 men. The fleet sailed south for two months. They made a 1,500-mile (2,400-km) crossing of the China Sea to Vietnam. On the island of Java, a center of the spice trade, they were held up for months by the torrential rains of the monsoon season.

They may also have encountered pirates here as the seas around the island were filled with them. They then traveled northwest to the Andaman Islands and a thousand miles (1,600 km) across the Bay of Bengal to Sri Lanka. They sailed up the coast of India and, still hugging the coast, around the Indian Ocean before arriving at Hormuz.

1294
The Polos deliver Princess Kokachin to Kerman. She marries Ghazan, new ruler of the Khanate of Persia.

1294
Kublai Khan dies.

Two years had passed since they set sail. On the way, nearly 600 people, including passengers and sailors, had died from storms, accidents, pirate attacks, and disease. Only one of the Persian ambassadors survived the journey. Fortunately, neither the Polos nor any of the ladies traveling in the fleet were lost. But as before, Hormuz was bad luck for the Polos. Here, they learned that Arghun, the bridegroom to be, had died. This meant that the princess they had been traveling with and protecting for two years had no one to marry.

The Persian ambassador and the Polos discussed the problem with the messengers who brought the bad news. The solution they came to was that the dead man's son, Ghazan, would marry Kokachin. The Polos escorted the young princess through Persia to Kerman, where the new groom was waiting. Kokachin was unhappy to let the three Venetians go and cried when they left.

So the Polos turned almost reluctantly toward home. It was now that they received a severe blow. They heard that Kublai Khan had died. He was 79 years old. With his death, a shadow fell over all of Central Asia. The golden age of the Mongol Empire was over. For the Polos, there would be no going back to China.

Pirates!

Highly organized pirates patrolled the seas of Southeast Asia. Twenty or thirty ships would work together in the search for merchant vessels. The pirates sailed with a gap of 5 or 6 miles (8–10 km) between each ship and could cover approximately a hundred miles (160 km) of sea. If one of them sighted a merchant ship, they would make a smoke signal and all the other pirate ships would attack the unlucky merchants and steal everything they had.

1295
Ghazan converts to Islam.

1295
The Polos arrive in Venice.

The Travelers Return

It took the Polos many months to reach Venice from Kerman. The three men were used to the magnificence of the cities of China. The towns and cities they now traveled through were nowhere near as grand. They had not seen Venice for 24 years. Since he was last there, Marco Polo had grown from a boy of 15 to a man of 39.

Above: A portrait of Marco Polo in old age taken from a wall painting by Varese made in the 16th century.

At last, the Polos arrived at their house in the Venetian quarter known as Cannaregio. They knocked on the door and demanded to be let in. A serving girl leaning out of a window did not know who they were. It took a long time to convince the family that these rough-looking men in their worn traveling clothes truly were Niccolo, Maffeo, and Marco. At last they were let in, and a story has grown up about what happened next.

A family dinner was held to celebrate their homecoming. The three men, still in their ragged clothes, did not look as if they had been making their fortune for all those years.

1298
Marco is captured by the Genoese. He begins to dictate the story of his travels.

1299
Marco is released from prison. Copies of his book start to circulate.

At last, the Polos stood up and took off their padded jackets. To their relatives' surprise, they took their knives and slashed at the seams of the old clothes. A stream of diamonds, emeralds, rubies, topazes, and sapphires scattered across the dining table. Here were the results of more than 20 years of trading, along with gifts from Kublai Khan. The Polos were very wealthy men indeed.

We know little more about the rest of Marco's life. The records of the city mention him only a few times. He married a rich Venetian called Donata Badoer and had three daughters: Fantina, Bellala, and Moreta. He continued to trade from Venice. In 1298, he commanded a battleship for the Venetians against Genoa in a war over who ruled the trade routes around the Mediterranean Sea. He was captured and imprisoned but was able to send a message to his father to send him his notebooks. In prison Marco began to tell of his adventures.

Marco died in 1324, aged 70. By this time he was no longer a rich man. In his will, he left what he had

Above: On January 9, 1324 Marco Polo made his will, leaving his few remaining possessions to his three daughters.

to his three daughters. He also ordered that his slave, Peter, a Mongol who had traveled back with him, should be set free. When Marco was dying his friends begged him to confess that the stories he had told in his book were not true. They were afraid that he would die with a lie on his conscience. He replied: "I have only told the half of what I saw."

Circa 1300
Marco marries Donata Badoer and they have three daughters.

1324
Marco Polo dies in Venice.

Marco's Legacy

Above: Bank notes had been in widespread use in China since the 10th century. They were first issued because carrying around a lot of precious metals to pay for goods was cumbersome and dangerous. Bank notes were not issued in Europe until 1660. This bank note is from Kublai Khan's first issue of paper money in 1260.

There is no record of what Marco Polo looked like; whether he was kind or bad-tempered; or even if he married in China. All these things will remain mysteries. What really matters is the great legacy that he left behind.

Marco Polo was by no means the first traveler to have made the journey he did. But he was the first to record in such detail the route through towns and cities in Persia, past the Pamir Mountains, across the Gobi Desert, along rivers and ravines to China. He told us not only a wonderful story of adventure and courage but also left an amazing record for traders and travelers coming after him. With his trader's eye, he described the places in which riches could be found. He also warned of the human and natural dangers on the way.

Marco Polo was the first European traveler to describe the fascinating world of China and the East. He was the very first European to mention Japan. He also mentions Tibet, Myanmar, Laos, Vietnam, India, Sumatra, and Sri Lanka. He wrote of the customs, lifestyles, daily life, and goods of the people he met.

1368
The Mongols are driven out of China.

1477
The first printed edition of *The Description of the World* is made.

Left: This European map of China made in 1459 was based on Marco Polo's descriptions of Kublai Khan's empire. Marco was the first European traveler to write about China.

He was the first Westerner to write of coal, paper money, and gunpowder. From him, Europeans first learned about the making of porcelain.

The Description of the World was the fullest account of the world written by a European up to that time. It opened Western eyes to the world beyond their own. It began a European fascination with the East that remains to this day. Marco's book encouraged others to journey beyond the known world.

One hundred and fifty years after Marco Polo's death, a sea captain from Genoa heard about the book and was fascinated. He decided to find the wonders Marco wrote about. He particularly longed to find Japan, which Marco had described as being rich in gold. He decided to sail around the world on a westward journey, in order to come to Japan from the east. The captain's name was Christopher Columbus. He didn't find Japan, but the Genoese sea captain did reach the Americas.

1492
Christopher Columbus reaches the Americas.

2006
The Silk Road has become a popular tourist route.

Glossary

ambassador an official sent by a king or a state as a representative to a foreign court.

bamboo a tropical plant of the grass family.

barter to exchange goods for other goods.

besiege to surround a town and force the people inside to surrender.

brigand someone who lives by robbery and kidnapping.

Buddhist someone who follows the teachings of Buddha (c.566–480 B.C.), who believed that human beings face endless reincarnations (rebirths and deaths) unless they gain release through wisdom and peace.

Byzantine Empire the eastern part of the Roman Empire, created when the Roman Empire collapsed. It lasted from A.D. 330 to 1453.

canal an artificial water course.

caravanserai an inn found on the great routes across the Middle East and Asia.

cardinals the most senior members of the Roman Catholic Church, after the pope.

circa around; used when referring to an approximate date or time.

convoy a group of supply ships escorted and protected by a group of warships.

crusades wars waged by Christian armies in the Middle Ages to take the Holy Land from the Muslims who ruled it.

dhow a sailing ship built of wood and used mainly in the Arabian Sea.

dictator an unelected ruler who keeps total power over the people he or she rules.

djin an ill-meaning spirit found in Arab myths and stories.

doge the title of the ruler of Venice in Marco Polo's time.

dynasty a family of rulers.

embalm to preserve dead bodies using sweet-smelling spices.

envoy an official messenger who is sent by one territory to another.

exotic foreign in a way that is exciting.

galleon a large sailing ship.

galley a long ship powered mainly by oars.

Genoa a port in Italy. In Marco Polo's time it was a powerful independent state that competed with Venice for control of trade routes around the Mediterranean Sea.

goblet a bowl-shaped drinking vessel without handles.

gondola a light boat used in Venice to transport people along the canals. A gondolier uses a long pole to push the boat along the canal.

guild a society, usually of craftspeople, set up for their own mutual aid.

Holy Land the region on the eastern shore of the Mediterranean, where Christ lived and died. It is also the homeland of the Jews and the site of places holy to Muslims.

hub the center of a wheel; also used to describe a city which is the focus of various trade routes.

junk sailing boat used in Chinese seas.

khanate one of the four regions of the Mongol Empire, ruled over by a khan, or chief.

lacquer a strong layer of varnish.

lagoon a saltwater lake on the coast, nearly surrounded by sandbanks.

Middle Ages the period of European history from around A.D. 1000 to A.D. 1500; also known as the medieval period.

Mongol referring to a people from the region of Mongolia in Central Asia. The Mongols were originally nomads who worshipped a number of nature gods. In the early 13th century, under the leadership of Genghis Khan and his successors, they began to create the largest empire the world has ever known.

mosaic a picture made by laying small colored pieces of stone or glass side by side.

Muslim a follower of the religion of Islam who worships one God and honors the prophet Muhammad.

mythical referring to myths, legends, and fairy tales; not real.

Nestorian Christian a member of an Asian Christian church founded by Nestorius of Constantinople in the 5th century A.D.

nomad someone who moves their flocks from pasture to pasture and is continually on the move.

oasis a fertile and watered place in a desert.

papal legate a representative of the pope in a country outside Italy.

passport a document recommending that the bearer is protected by officials in countries through which they pass.

pirate someone who attacks ships at sea and robs them of everything they carry.

pope the head of the Roman Catholic Church. He is now based in the Vatican in Rome, Italy.

porcelain a high-quality china or crockery. The secret of its manufacture was kept by the Chinese potters who made it.

prostrate to show respect for a ruler by lying face down before them.

pyre a pile of logs on which the dead are burned, or cremated.

silk a cloth made from the fibers spun from the cocoon of the silkworm.

Silk Road a network of trade routes across Central Asia linking the Mediterranean in the west with China in the east. It developed in the 2nd century B.C.

yurt a felt tent that is still used by some Mongols today. It can be taken down easily and packed onto animals.

Zoroastrian a person who follows the religious teachings of the Persian prophet Zoroaster, who lived in the 7th and 6th centuries B.C.

Bibliography

Humble, Richard, *Marco Polo,* Weidenfeld & Nicolson, London, 1975

Jackson, Peter, *The Mongols and the West 1221–1410,* Longman, Harlow, Essex, 2005

Larner, John, *Marco Polo and the Discovery of the World,* Yale Nota Bene, New Haven, Connecticut, 2001

Polo, Marco, *The Travels of Marco Polo: The Complete Yule-Cordier Edition,* 2 volumes, Dover Publications, Mineola, NY, 1993

Wood, Frances, *Did Marco Polo Go to China?,* Westview Press, New York, 1998

Wood, Frances, *The Silk Road: 2,000 Years in the Heart of Asia,* University of California Press, Berkeley, 2003

Sources of quotes:

p.37 *The Travels of Marco Polo: The Complete Yule-Cordier Edition,* Polo, Marco, 1993

p.49 *The Travels of Marco Polo: The Complete Yule-Cordier Edition,* Polo, Marco, 1993

Some Web sites that will help you to explore Marco Polo's world:

afe.easia.columbia.edu/mongols/
Resources about the Mongols and their empire.

www.metmuseum.org/explore/Marco/get_1.htm
Explore artifacts from the Metropolitan Museum of Art, New York, relating to Marco Polo's travels.

www.silk-road.com
Timelines on the Silk Road and Central Asia, plus articles on Marco Polo and trade.

Index

Acknowledgments

B = bottom, C = center, T = top, L = left, R = right.

Front cover Luisa Ricciarini Photo Agency/Luigino Visconti/Palazzo Tursi, Genoa; **1** Scala Archives, Florence/HIP/Oxford Science Archive; **3** The Art Archive; **7** AKG-images/Schutze/Rhodemann; **8** Scala Archives, Florence/Fondazione Querini Stampalia; **9** AKG-images/Cameraphoto; **11** AKG-images/ Bibliotheque Nationale, Paris; **12** John Heseltine; **13** Scala Archives, Florence; **14T** Scala Archives, Florence; **14B** AKG-images/Cameraphoto, Venice; **15T** Scala Archives, Florence/Museo dell'Arte Vetraria, Murano; **15B** Scala Archives, Florence/Museo Correr; **16** The Bridgeman Art Library/Musée Paul Dupuy/ Giraudon; **17** The Bridgeman Art Library/Bibliotheque Nationale, Paris; **19** Scala Archives, Florence/ Museo Civico, Bologna; **20–23** The Art Archive; **24T** British Library; **24B** AKG-images; **25** AKG-images/ Bibliotheque Nationale, Paris; **26** The Art Archive; **27** AKG-images/Bibliotheque Nationale, Paris; **29** The Art Archive/Bibliotheque Nationale, Paris; **30** AKG-images/Bibliotheque Nationale, Paris; **32** AKG-images/Bibliotheque Nationale, Paris; **35** Corbis/Reza/Webistan; **36** AKG-images/Bibliotheque Nationale, Paris; **38** Corbis/Alison Wright; **39** Scala Archives, Florence/British Museum, London; **40** Corbis/Steve Bein; **41** AKG-images/Bibliotheque Nationale, Paris; **43** The Bridgeman Art Library/ Museo Correr/Giraudon; **44** The Art Archive; **45** The Bridgeman Art Library/National Palace Museum, Taipei; **46–47** AKG-images/Bibliotheque Nationale, Paris; **48** Royal Asiatic Society; **49** AKG-images/ Musée Guimet, Paris; **51** The Art Archive; **52** AKG-images/Bibliotheque Nationale, Paris; **53** The Art Archive; **54** AKG-images/Bibliotheque Nationale, Paris; **56** The Bridgeman Art Library/Villa Farnese, Lazio; **57** The Bridgeman Art Library/Private Collection; **58** The Bridgeman Art Library/Private Collection; **59** The Art Archive/Biblioteca Nazionale Marciana, Venice.